Tears of

Jean Vanier

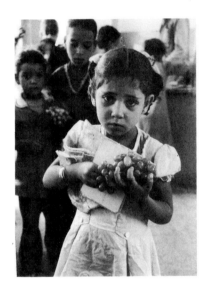

Darton, Longman and Todd
London

First published in Great Britain in 1973 by
Darton, Longman and Todd Ltd
89 Lillie Road, London SW6 1UD
© *Jean Vanier 1970 and 1991*

Fifth Printing 1982

Second edition 1991

British Library Cataloguing in Publication Data
Vanier, Jean
  Tears of silence – 2nd ed.
  1. English poetry
  I. Title
  821.914

  ISBN 0–232–51932–3

Printed and bound in Great Britain by
Courier International Ltd, Tiptree, Essex

Introduction

Tears of Silence was written in 1968. It flowed from my encounter with Raphael and Philippe and with many others who, like them, were intellectually disabled. Very quickly I discovered their cry for love, friendship and communion, a cry much deeper than the cry for success, wealth, a good job, recognition, prestige and honour which is found in so many other people.

And in that cry deep in the heart of the Raphaels and Philippes I met, I discovered the deepest cry in the heart of each and every human being for love, friendship and communion. At the same time, I discovered how very wounded we all are in our capacity to relate. We all yearn for love, yet are frightened of it. We thirst for friendship and communion, but tend to cling to others and thus we damage love. For love cannot be possessed. It is a gift; it is like a gentle breeze that brings deep, inner freedom to each person.

Both Raphael and Philippe had been abandoned in an asylum at the death of their parents. When I bought a house in 1964, and we began living together, I wanted to create a new type of family for them, a Christian community. This initial community has grown. There are now some four hundred people living in different houses scattered throughout Trosly and the neighbouring villages. L'Arche has also spread in other countries. In 1991, there are some ninety-five communities in all the continents and many new seeds have been planted and are beginning to grow. The cry for community and the needs for a place of welcome for intellectually disabled people are so great!

Throughout the years, I have also heard the cry of many parents. In 1971, during a pilgrimage to Lourdes which was especially for people with intellectual disabilities, their parents and friends, Faith and Light was born. There are now some nine hundred Faith and Light communities throughout the world which meet regularly to celebrate life together, to express their mutual commitment and to pray.

Tears of silence continue to be shed by so many people in our world today. There are so many men, women and children whose cry for love is left unheard, unrecognized. So often these silent tears are in the hearts of young people whose capacities of love have not yet been called forth. If the spring of love does not flow from our hearts, we tend to die.

The cry of the weak and of the poor in our world reveal to us the cry for love in others who are endowed with intellectual riches but do not know how to relate. May these two cries for love meet and call forth the waters of love in each other, in order to bring hope to a broken and divided world.

JEAN VANIER

Our lives are fleeting moments in which are found the seeds of eternal peace, unity and love as well as the seeds of war, dissension and indifference. When will we rise and awaken to the choice before each of us, to water and to give light to one or the other of these two seeds?
Must we accept damnation or can humanity be saved?

This book is dedicated to all those of the House of the Dying in Calcutta. It is dedicated to the faces that are shown here, faces and people who represent you and me, and all those who are fearful, and all those who aspire to universal brotherhood.

' grieve to speak of love and yet not love as I should.
 ask forgiveness of the many I have wounded
  nd of the many I have passed without seeing their wounds.
Pray for me, my brother.

How many times
      a meeting has struck barriers
          cement blocks
              in me
heart of stone
heart of stone
      unable to listen
     i fear
      and fly by
who can liberate me from myself?

he who clutches desperately to security —

    to every day habits, work, organization, friends,
                                           family . . . . .

        closed off . . . .

    no longer lives:

    more than security,

        life needs

                       adventure

                       risk

                       dynamic activity

                       self-giving

                       presence to others

in the paths of our existence

        there are at times obstacles . . . . . .

               rocks barring the road . . . . . .

if these obstacles appear too great

        or if we, through fatigue or other reasons,

           are deflated,

           then we sit and weep

               unable to advance . . . . . unable to
                                     return . . . . .

               some failure has damaged our
                         élan . . . .

               an unfaithful friend

               failure in exams

                   in work

             we no longer feel that blossoming dynamism

             we carry our bodies like lumps of lead,

                   lumps of lead,

             we slumber into a world of disillusionment

                 apathetic
                 listless

but then comes change

        winter changes to spring

         we meet a friend

          we rest

        forces awaken in our bodies

        life seems to surge once more . . . .

                      as the morning sun

                      calm
                      unswerving
                      certain
                      never faltering

.........others fall,

          sink into sadness,

            rise

              but fall again too quickly......

                 obstacle seems to follow obstacle

and they remain deflated....depressed....downhearted....

                                        crushed

  life does not seem to blossom......

          the joy of living has fled

              maybe never was

from depression

          they are sucked into despair

from sadness

          into misery

....alone

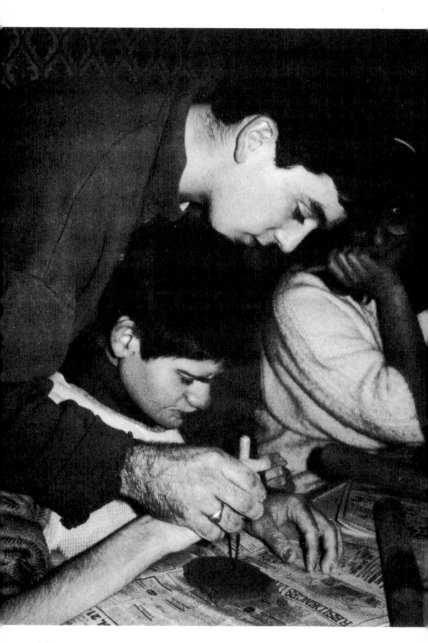

the man in misery is crushed. . . . . encircled

without hope of rising by himself

surrounded and knotted with obstacles and
difficulties. . . . .

no desire

no hope

no motivation

no will to live

closed off

man is a marvelous and mysterious being

when called forth

calling forth

strength

tenderness

can surge up in him

giving life

and then there can be a bursting forth of quiet energy. . . . . .

capacity for creativity. . . . . . generosity. . . . . . deep

attention. . . . . . concern. . . . . . work. . . . . . a sense of

wonderment. . . . . . some taste of the infinite. . .

never ceasing. . . . evolving. . . . deepening. . .

creating. . . . . . calling. . . . . .

when something interests me
how easy it becomes
vital . . . . . living
no interest . . . . . apathy
i wander down life's path
cynical
and sad
sad unto death
how quickly i die
who will call me forth?

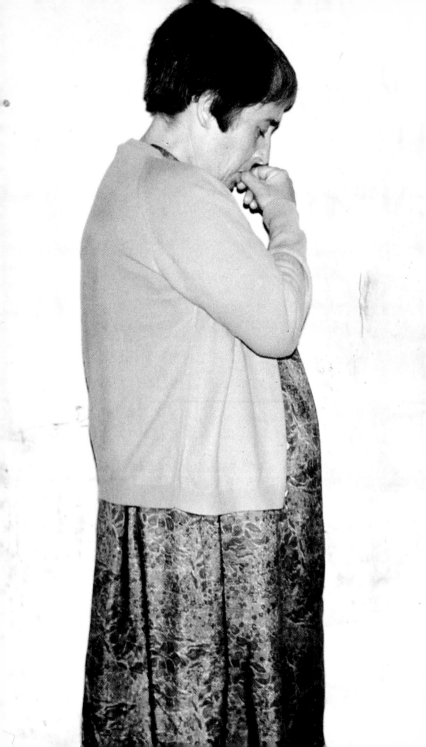

being down......with no life

        no beauty

            that beauty which flows with life......

                              eyes....

                           living eyes...

           not radiating

               no longer a source of attraction....

                  nothing in me attracts....

               people turn away their eyes.....

i am not only dejected

          but rejected

          covered with shame

              deserted...abandoned...

                        alone.....in anguish

              crucified

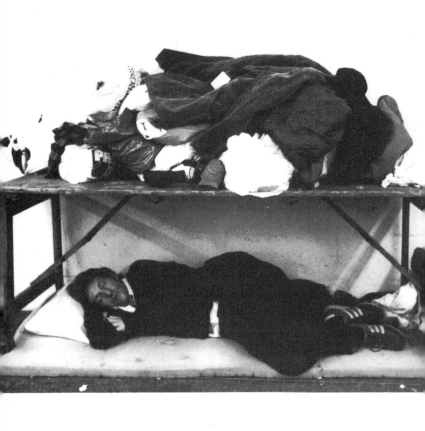

i who am dejected
        let go that inner hold......
                sink down......down.....
        friends drift downstream
                        laughing....
i remain......lying on my bed
                smoking
                drinking
            or sitting....sitting
                the radio playing on and on and on
            waiting
            waiting
                but waiting for
                    what.....

and i am afraid......

      those haggard eyes

         or open wounds

         or black skin or white skin

         or alcoholic smell

         or freaked out mind

           of the man in misery

        strike deep chords of fear within me....

    fear of losing my money, time, reputation, liberty

      fear, above all, of losing myself

        fear of the unknown,

           for misery is a world of the unknown.....

        terror of despair,

           those hands.... those hands.....

           those hands stretched out towards
                        me....

           i am afraid to touch them......

             they may drag me down, down,

             down to some unknown
                future........

i fear my helplessness

     my hollows

        my poverty

you remind me that i too must die

and so i turn my back

     returning to my home

        escaping the fundamental reality

          of my own existence,

            of my own poverty

              and yours, my brother.....

        i refuse to love......

because i fear your grasping hand
                    calling me to the unknown
                        the unknown of love
because i fear my emptiness
                my poverty
                my call to death
        i fear myself
        i close my heart . . . . . cement block . . .
                    shut myself off
                        from you,
                            my despairing brother
you are in a prison of despair, sadness . . .
i too am in prison
    but my bars and locks
        are my so-called friends, clubs, social conventions,
            "what everybody else is doing" . . .
barriers that i have built
        that prevent me seeing you,
                my brother
your presence,
        miserable, sad . . .
            is a call . . . .
                do i turn away
                    or do i dare . . . . .
love is the greatest of all risks
        to give myself . . . . to you
            do i dare . . . . do i dare
                leap into the cool, swirling, living waters
                    of loving fidelity

.....the miserable man is still there
waiting...waiting....waiting for what
lying in his prison....
lying in his dung.....
waiting
yet
not waiting
for he has lost hope
we only wait when there is hope
where there is no hope......we lie.....dying
not living
sad unto death
yet he waits
waiting.............yet not waiting

the worthy lady, over rimmed glasses, saying:
  "lazy"
the bank manager shouting:
  "stupid"
are right . . . . in a way . . . .
the miserable man knows it only too well
his misery is the awareness of his misery
  "i remain in the vomit of my worthlessness . . . . . "

he knows this worthlessness
    and has lost hope
the man in misery is not ignorant
only lacking in strength . . . . vitality
that which springs from hope
        and he has no hope . . . . . .
his misery is greater because of his awareness
        therein lies his despair
        he cannot rise
        not feeling worthy to rise

the person in misery does not need a look that
        judges and criticizes
        but a comforting presence
            that brings peace and hope and life
            and says:
                "you are a human person
                    important
                    mysterious
                    infinitely precious
                what you have to say
                    is important
                    because it flows
                        from a human person
                in you there are those seeds
                        of the infinite
                        those germs of love...of beauty
                        which must rise from the earth
                                            of your misery
                    so humanity be fulfilled.
            if you do not rise
                then something will be missing
                if you are not fulfilled
                    it is terrible
                        you must rise again
                            on the third day.....
                rise again because we all need
                you
                for you are a child of God
                you, sam
                            john
                                    willie mae
                        my brother....my sister
                            be loved
                            beloved"

In some mysterious way
      the quality of my presence my look
            brings to you life

          or death

that look......

      that hand......

           calls forth

                life....hope....joy...

if

you believe in me

then maybe

i can do something worthwhile......

    maybe i am worthwhile

maybe i can do something with my life

thus

the light of hope begins to burn

   your constant trust in me

      communicates warm sensations of confidence

         and faith

    that look in your eyes

       the touch of your hands

           brings me some marvellous message of hope

"your slightest look easily will unclose me
though i have closed myself as fingers,
you open always petal by petal as Spring comes
(touching skilfully, mysteriously) her first
rose"

                    e. e. cummings

how then to approach the miserable child
        not haughtily
                    but humbly
        not judging but loving
                    determined not to dominate
                    not even to give things
                    rather to give myself
                            my time
                                    energy
                            and heart

and to listen
            believing that he is important
                a child of God
                        in whom Jesus lives

approach with tenderness
            gently

gently giving one's friendship
            delicate soothing hands
                bearing the oil of mercy
                    annointing deep wounds

"A new heart will I give you
 and a new spirit I will put within
 you and I will take out of your
 flesh the heart of stone and give
 you a heart of flesh."
                    (ezechiel 36:26)

he who is

or has been

deeply hurt

has a RIGHT

to be sure

he is

L O V E D

love!
>not just some passing moment
>>a glance however open
but some deeper compassion
>>radiating permanency
not some morbid curiosity
>some gushing pity
>>incompetent naiveté

the cry of burnt-out eyes
>>wounded bodies
>addicted minds
>>cravings
can only be answered by some deeper love
>in which is felt a strange presence of the eternal
>>a hope
>>a new security
not some passing glance
>but deeper bonds
>>unbreakable

com-passion

        is a meaningful word . . . . .

        sharing the same passion

           the same suffering

           the same agony

              accepting in my heart

                the misery in yours, o, my brother

                and you, accepting me

o yes there is fear

        but even more deeply

        there is the insistent cry from the entrails of the
                            suffering one

           that calls me forth . . . . .

        some faint feeling

           of confidence

        that my smile . . . . . . my presence

      has value and can give

           life

thus deep friendship is born

                mutual presence
                humble and forgiving
           engendering

                  quiet joy
                  fidelity

but

who will bring life to

the despairing,

to crushed and dying hearts

to those whose future is barred

to the mentally sick

to the aged and alone

to the despised and anguished

to the burnt out

statesmen are called upon to enact laws

but who is called to give hope to the despairing

how to approach him

he, repulsive and fearful

i, with my fear and my security

and yet......

i feel.....in some mysterious way

that there is a calling

the silent crying out of misery

tears of silence

and in my deepest being i hear this call

a sort of whispering

that life has meaning, but

in the degree that i find love

no reasons.....no reasons why......only a sort of.....

an act.....

an act of faith that i can enter into some vast and powerful

movement

of life and life giving

. . . . that my joy gives joy
my hope gives hope
and

that i can communicate in some silent way
the spirit living in me
not by what i say
but how i say it

a deep concern
a way of listening
to the faint heart beats
of your existence and life

42

listening
l i s t e n i n g
l i s t e n i n g

        whispering
        silent
        a listening that comforts
            and calls forth

DO I DARE
do i dare
    believe
       your silent call
         your tears of silence

but there is the world of efficiency
               techniques
               diplomas
               business (and business is business!)

and then there are my friends
      who think i'm crazy . . . . . are they friends?
                am i crazy?

. . . . DOUBTS . . . . . .

conflicting forces
        fatigue
        fears

and yet life calls forth
        compassion in my entrails

this strange and silent war
      do i dare
      do i dare
        believe
      do i dare
      do i dare

        surrender myself to your call

43

"if you pour yourself out for the hungry
and satisfy the desire of the afflicted
then shall your light rise in the darkness
and your gloom be as the noonday
and the Lord will guide you continually

and you shall be like a watered garden
like a spring of water
whose waters fail not."

isaiah 58

o God
 my God
   keep me from flinching/waning
       slumbering into that timeless rest
           that never is
keep me from falling into a prison
           of egotistical habits
               where the bars
               are superficial friends
                   and drinks
                   and stupid laughter
                   kisses without love
                   business and organisation
                       without heart
                   and gifts for self-flattery
           these bars that prevent life evolving
               towards that taste of the infinite
                   open to your call . . . .

break down those barriers
       that prevent me living, my God,
break down those barriers
       that threaten to stifle me . . . .

barriers broken down too quickly

     are

          another form

            of death......

        too much exposure

        too much cold

those who have learned life too quickly

    have thus lost life

those who have thrown themselves into

            experiences of sexuality

            drugs for escape

       but who have lost life :

               presence

               communion

        because love grows

            is a deepening fusion of peace

                    and liberty

i fear

the mysterious power of compassion

i

do not

believe in it

because that implies having found myself

that i no longer play

play a game

put on a mask — a personage

pretending to be

appearing

but that i become myself

accepting my poverty

letting the Spirit breathe

move
live
love

in me

opening my being
(no fear)

to the delicate touch

of His hand that opens me

but i fear

and wear my mask

maturity of the heart:

        accepting

        myself

                with my limits

                in my poverty

                i do not fear

                        the

                        other

no fear that

                i will be eaten up

                devoured

                lose my being

no fear

                of showing who i am

in each of us there is a need to

L I V E

the flowering out of life
the thirst for beautiful things

the feel of my radiance
in joy
in hope

in each of us there is a need to live

but also

there are those seeds of death

no will to live

no desire to get up in the morning

never able to sleep. . . . always wanting
to sleep. . . . .

but never sleeping

always down

and criticizing

no zest or energy

just-every-day-doing-what-i-must

with no zing

or laughter

i need to feel

        i am

        i am unique

            capable of love and life

                not just one of the crowd

                    looking towards life

                        but myself living. . . . .

i must not remain in a sort of

                        non-life

                        non-existence

                        closed in

                        despairing

            for this can be a taste of death. . . . . . .

life is a flowering vine . . . . .

        too much light . . . . . . or too little

        too much water . . . . . . or too little

brings blight and death . . . . burnt-up, dried up, drowned . . . . . .

life needs delicate gentle hands, hands that know

just the right amount of water for life

just the right degree of light

at the right time . . . .

or else, no life, no flower, no fruit . . . .

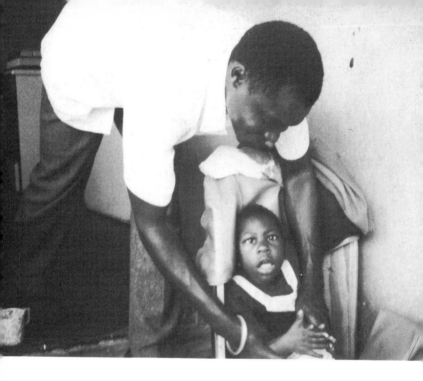

to evolve
      life does need security
            in the mother
            in the father
            in the home
                with friends

        but above all trust in the spirit
           against all assaults of fear and anguish
           against all the unknowns
           against anything that might destroy
                  the flowering of my life...

the biological movement

of growth

needs

this physical and spiritual

complement of love

and so to evolve

the child

needs

the look

the hands

of his mother

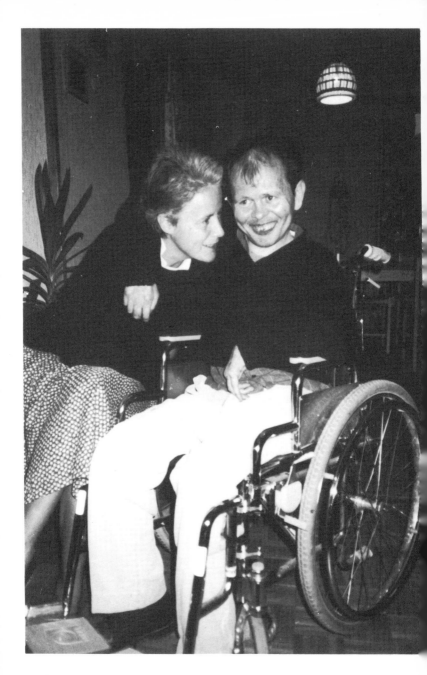

life needs

        security and hope

security being
the fundamental basis

        the earth

           in which life is born

hope being
that call . . . . . to light

        and love

          and beauty

        . . . . . . universality

        shadows of the infinite

risk

and hope

love of the unknown

passionate interest in the present

thirst for adventure

desire for new experiences

outpourings of generosity

quest for knowledge

openness to the future

call to love

availability to the Spirit

peaceful contemplation

high skies

mountains

deep lakes

deep breathing

wonderment

love is the greatest of all risks

the giving of myself

but do i dare take this risk
diving into the cool
swirling
living waters of

LOVING FIDELITY

an encounter

               is a strange

                   and wonderful thing

presence

one person to another

present

one to another

    life flowing

        one to another

but

we can be together
             and not meet

we can live in the same house day after day
             sit at the same table
             kneel at the same pew.
             read the same books
                  but never meet

we can kiss
             gestures of love
             apparent tenderness
                  but never meet

a meeting is a strange and wonderful thing

presence one person to another
             present one to another
             life flowing one to another

.......but to listen
                    to listen intently

my God i wish i could listen
                            to my brother

listen to his heart beats

listen to those faint...o so faint...
                    calls
                    which are there
                    hidden

under.....i know not why....
                    some sort of fear

listening
                    but instead
                        i have my own ideas
                        and i penetrate
                        destroying
                        harvesting all that is there

to make bread
                        for i
                        for me
                        for myself

i need to talk

       and walk

            with another

i need to express myself

       say things. . . . .

this is a movement of life

       life that is in me

            and needs to flow out. . . .

i must speak. . . . . and dance

       sharing things i love and hate

            my hopes, my joys, my fears, my griefs. . .

     giving myself

     giving my life

     giving life

a tiny child needs not only food and shelter

                but something more . . . much more . . . .

    a feeling of love

    that someone cares for him

        ready to die for him

    that he is really loved

    that he is important . . . . precious

      and so he begins to live

        begins to sense the value of his being

and so it is that life rises in him

    and he grows in confidence

        in himself

        and in his possibilities of life

            and of creation

effort

       conceived.....

          born...

             and nurtured

                in love

e miserable man   t
eat you as a stranger....   w
u were born and reared in   o
                squalor...
u are walled in, for you have   p
                    no life   r
front of you.....no joys to   i
                    look   s
ward to....no loving   o
                children....   n
   esteem   s

                          d
                          i
                          v   i, with my clean clothes, my
                          i   sensitive nose (i hate bad
                          d   smells)
                          e   my politeness....a warm
                          d   house...
                                       a world of security...the light
                               b   of reality does not penetrate my
                               y   cell, the reality of human
                                                                 misery
                                       so widespread, so deep.....
                          a

                          g
                          u
                          l
                          f

         two prisons divided by a gulf: the miserable
                                   man......
         and, imprisoned in the cell next door, the man
                                        of means
         comfortably installed.....and so the world
                                         goes on,
         and the gulf gets wider

                who will be the bridge

"i do not want to be reborn

    but if that should happen

        i would like to find myself amongst the untouchables

            in order to share their affliction,

                their sufferings

                and the insults they are subject to.

in this way,

    perhaps i would have the chance

        to liberate them and myself

            from this miserable condition."

gandhi

two worlds that never meet
        divided by a gulf called fear.....

who can assuage this fear

who can heal the wounds of this fear
              riches will not bring comfort
                  to the man without hope....
          he needs the warm light of confidence
             a will to live.... he knows his misery
                he is too convinced of his
                    apparent worthlessness
          what he lacks is not knowledge
          rather the hope and strength
            to rise from the filth.....

where to find this strength
       springing from hope
              which will conquer fear?

"blessed are the merciful

for they shall obtain mercy"

jesus

Acknowledgements

Thanks are due to the following for permission to reproduce their photographs:

Crisis: pp. 8; 10; 18; 20; 22; 26; 35; 40; 50; 54; 64; 66; 72 (photographs on pp. 10; 18; 20; 40; 54; 72 are by Neil Libbert; photograph on p. 35 is by David Hoffman).

L'Arche: pp. 6; 12; 14; 16; 32; 36; 38; 42; 43; 48; 49; 52; 53; 56; 57; 58; 61; 62; 65; 70; 78.

The United Nations Relief and Works Agency: pp. 1; 27; 28; 30; 34; 50; 55; 68; 74; 76 (photographs on pp. 1; 27; 68; 74 are by George Nehmeh; photographs on pp. 28; 30; 34; 55 are by Munir Nasr; photograph on p. 76 is by H. Haider).

Donna Moyseuik: pp. 7; 24.

Christine Amer: pp. 44; 46.

Morag Reeve: p. 60.